T0193613

ÀPÈKÉ

BOOK 1: ÀPÈKÉ IS BORN!

Called To Be Treasured

Story by **Mofolusho Rosanwo**

WestBow Press books may be ordered
through booksellers or by contacting:

WestBow Press
A Division of Thomas Nelson & Zondervan
1663 Liberty Drive
Bloomington, IN 47403
www.westbowpress.com
844-714-3454

EDITORS Rev Táyò Shódípò, Deacon Emmanuel Shótálà

Pictures and Illustrations are copyright belonging to
iStock
The Olátúnjís
The Olánírans
The Rósanwós
The Awósémòs

The Shótálàs
The Oláògúns

All are very supportive that the project must be
successfully completed. These images cannot be
reused without the permission of the owners.

ISBN: 979-8-3850-1578-8 (sc)
ISBN: 979-8-3850-1579-5 (e)

Library of Congress Control Number: 2023924613

Print information available on the last page.

WestBow Press rev. date: 01/18/2024

Contents

Preface

Àpèké means "Called to be treasured". Mofólúshó means 'I commit to The Lord's care'. Ọmóbólá, 'Child born into prosperity (or wealth)'. And Monísọlá,'I have a share in prosperity'. They are all Yorùbá names (the Author's names) from western Nigeria, West Africa. The original little Àpèké appears riding her tricycle towards the end of this story. She was not born on a Sunday. That was an addendum to start an interesting discussion on Yorubas and Sundays. Her junior brother in real life is Olúfémi Àrèmú Adélęgàn. Yorùbá accents are difficult because some words are shortened with repeated use over many years. Like, Adélęgàn should in full be Adéòlęgàn, meaning the crown cannot be mocked. This might explain the difficulty placing signs on many names. Also pronounciations occasionally differ. Some say Yorùbá, and some say Yòrùbá. The meaning is the same.

The Milestone later in the story can be described as prophetic or only imaginary (God knows. We just have to wait!).

Abbreviations

OFNC Overseas Fellowship of Nigerian Christians

Dedication

To God, My Redeemer, Healer, Lover of my soul, Teacher and Deliverer

My Parents, Mr Shadrack Titus Adélẹ̀gàn and Mrs Eunice Ọlákúǹbi Adélẹ̀gàn wonderful parents. Both late, and my beautiful Aunt, Mrs Mopélọ́lá Ajíbọ́lá, who continued to parent, pray for, and encourage me.

My Beloved Late Husband, Dr. Emmanuel Rósanwó, my best friend and encourager.

My Son, Dr Samuel Rósanwó, my best gift ever, and his beautiful family.

Acknowledgements

Pat, my swimming club friend, who first inspired me to write my story in 1993/94.

Rev Dr Johnson & Rev Dr Doyin Abímbọ́lá, our Pastors, who encouraged me to get going in 2010/11.

Dr Mrs Sayò Ọdẹ́jídé, Rev Táyò Shódípọ̀, Mrs Eileen Kermode, Dr Zac Adélẹ̀yẹ, Dr Mrs Afiniki Ònílarí, Mrs Rónkẹ́ Adégòkè, Mrs Augusta Ògúnyẹmí, Mr. Ṣèyí Joseph and Dr Bímbọ́ Ọlániran who read through and suggested modifications.

Tutor, Knowsley Community College, Chris Cole, who did a project of writing a story book for children with us.

OFNC Over 50s group and Liverpool OFNC group for financial support, moral and prayer support.

Library Staff, Knowsley Community College, for their big help with the initial formatting of the document.

Dr & Dr Mrs Bímbọ́ & Tóbi Ọláníran, Dr & Mrs Tolú and Bísí Àkànmú, Dr & Mrs Tọ́lá and Jùmọ̀ké Awósẹ́mọ̀, Dr & Mrs Lánre & Adéwùnmí Ọ̀ké yà, Mr & Mrs Dàpọ̀ and Rónké Ọlátúnjí, Mr & Mrs Tolú and Táíwò Oláògún, Deacon Emmanuel and Deaconess Kẹ́misọ́lá Shótálà, Mrs Bùnmi Àràoyè and their families for tremendous help with photography, encouragement, and painstaking search for excellent images.

Author's parents

Below Dr & Mrs Tolú and Bísí Àkànmú lLiverpool OFNC. They were determined the project should not be abandoned.

ÀPÈKẸ́ IS BORN!

It was in the early hours of Sunday. The loud cry typical of labour rooms, and a baby is born in Ìbàdàn, a city in Nigeria.

Illustration1 Nigeria in Africa

Illustration 2 Ìbàdàn in Nigeria

Sunday, the day she was born, is a special day when Christians come together to worship God. The baby has beautiful curly black hair. What a big relief for mother after the labour pains.

Illustration 3: Baby with Beautiful curly black hair

The whole family was happy and there was excitement when mother and baby came home. Soon it's time to feed again and baby is breastfed happily by mother, big sister savouring the joy of the moment.

Illustration 4: mother breastfeeding her baby

The baby is called '' Túnfúlú" (meaning ''new flesh" in Yorùbá language) or ''Aròbó" for a week; or simply '' àbúrò", meaning junior, until she gets named by Dad, Mum, Grandparents, Uncles, Aunties on the 8ᵗʰ day - that's right; each likely bringing his or her own name selection. That is Yorùbá custom. Pastor and family friends are also in attendance. One of the names this baby is given is ÀPÈKẸ́. It means ''Called to be treasured". It is a Yorùbá name, and in this instance, a pet name or ''oríkì". Another name she came with by reason of the day of birth, Sunday, is "Abọ́sẹ̀dé". Sunday is called 'Ọjọ́ Ọ̀sẹ̀ or Ọjọ́ Ìsinmi' in Yorùbá . "Abọ́sẹ̀dé" means 'came on a Sunday'. It is a girl's name. Boys are called ''Sunday" similarly if born on a Sunday. There is a Yorùbá song about Sunday. The English meaning is in parenthesis.

Ọ̀sẹ̀ ọ̀sẹ̀ rere	[Sunday, wonderful day]
Ìwo ọjọ́ 'sinmi	[Day of rest]
Ó ye k'á f'ìyìn ọlá	[We ought to give praise and honour]
Fún Ọlọ́run lókè	[To God in heaven above]

Now this is all in relation to the Yorùbás, a people group occupying the bulk of the Southwest of Nigeria and scattered by trade and commerce into many other West African countries. They are found amongst Nigerian and African migrants in Europe, America and all over the world.

Other people groups in West Africa also have their own infant naming ceremony customs, which are often tied up with religious beliefs of great great grandparents and those gone before. For example, some pour out libations to invoke gods and ancestors that have passed away. Families need to know in these days of interracial marriages; that we need to remember and honour our ancestors, and there are not a few brave men and women. They should

however never be worshipped as gods, or their spirits invoked. This is idolatry, which is contrary to the Christian doctrine.

For it is written, 'You shall worship the Lord your God, and Him only you shall serve'''
-Luke 4:8 New King James Version (NKJV)

Yorùbá Christians use the opportunity of the naming ceremony to bless the child and the family. There is singing and Bible reading. The Pastor who officiates encourages and guides the parents as to the best ways to bring him or her up in the knowledge and love of God. In the past, it was common practice for him to give the baby certain symbolic food items to taste like Sugar, Honey, Salt, Water. As he gives each item, he says something like:

- as sugar sweetens, may this child's life sweeten lives she touches in Jesus Name;

- as honey is sweet, may the journey of life for this child be a pleasant one, in Jesus Name;

- As palm oil soothes and lubricates, may God by His Holy Spirit smoothen life's journey for this child, in Jesus Name.

- As water is universal and has no enemies, may this child be welcome everywhere she goes, in Jesus Name

- As salt preserves and purifies, may this child maintain truth, justice and righteousness everywhere she goes, in Jesus Name.

As we can all see, infant naming is very important to the Yorùbás; which is why the ceremony is classically done first thing in the morning around 6 or 7 am. Blessings on all [Kúàárò] Kaaro Oòjíire people for that diligence. However, we should ask ourselves, is such diligence widely reflected in regular community and work life in present day Nigeria,

Yorùbá land included? In truth, it is not. One can only conclude even though a proud Yorùbá; that our ceremonies, without accompanying trust in Christ, faithful discipleship, community action putting heads together to solve problems; can only get us so far. Not very far really. May The Lord help and guide us all, in Jesus's Name! His grace is forever sufficient for His own. Amen. So, let's continue with our description of the Naming Ceremony.

In the days when everyone lived in the same community; paternal grandparents, maternal grandparents, parents, uncles and aunties were obliged to attend. As each one announces his or her choice of name, a monetary gift is deposited for the baby. Coin currency was deposited in a clean, beautiful dish of water – not anymore, as most cash is paper now. Everyone in attendance has the opportunity to give cash as the dish is passed around, concurrently as the baby's name is pronounced, to show their goodwill. Then a meal is served and enjoyed together. Many Yorùbá Christians don't give their babies food items to taste any more during their naming ceremony, so avoiding any links with the religion of their ancestors.

Illustration 5: coins in bowl of water

Illustration 6: naming ceremony group

If they are of another religion, they will follow their own faith to pray. Although Yorùbás need greater strength to cope when we are faced with challenges and disability, all babies are treasured.

YOU ARE
TREASURED **TOO**
WHEREVER YOU ARE BORN

WHETHER IN AFRICA

Illustration 7: Children from Africa

OR EUROPE

Illustration 8: Children from Europe

OR SOUTH AMERICA

Illustration 9: Children from South America

OR ANYWHERE ELSE THE WORLD OVER

Illustration 10a: A Child from Asia

Illustration 10B: Children from Asia

JESUS CARES ABOUT YOU

Whether in the cold winter

Or a warm and sunny day

JESUS LOVES YOU JUST THE SAME

HE LOVES AND TREASURES EVERYONE,
WHATEVER YOUR FAVOURITE FOOD OR GARMENT.

Illustration 12: Family Eating

For God so loved the world that He gave His Only Son, so that
everyone who believes in him may not die but have eternal life.
John 3:16 GNB

GOD LOVES ME_____(Put your name here)

JESUS LOVES YOU WHETHER YOU ARE HELPING IN THE KITCHEN

Illustration 13: Boy Helping in the Kitchen

OR IN THE SHED

Illustration 14: Boy Doing Carpentry

OR PLAYING WITH YOUR FRIENDS

Illustration 15 A and B: Children Playing

JESUS SAYS I AM SPECIAL!

Illustration 16: Boy Drumming

I AM FEARFULLY AND WONDERFULLY MADE.

(Parent, please read Psalm 139:13-16 to child)

For you created my inmost being;
you knit me together in my mother's womb.
I praise you because I am fearfully and wonderfully made;
your works are wonderful, I know that full well.
My frame was not hidden from you when I was made in the secret place,
when I was woven together in the depths of the earth.
Your eyes saw my unformed body;
all the days ordained for me were written in your book before one of them came to be.
Psalm 139:13-16 (NIV)

God makes a plan for each child to be a blessing. He made me with a special plan for my life like in these 2 pages of a book.

April 1, 2011	Born in Ibadan, Nigeria
May 2, 2011	First Smile
September 20, 2011	Sitting milestone
December 30, 2011	Crawling milestone
March 20, 2012	Stands unaided
April 3, 2012	Walking milestone
October 4, 2014	Starts School
April 5, 2017	Accepts Christ as Saviour, name is written in the book of life
April 4, 2020	Starts singing in the choir
July 20, 2032	Becomes a Doctor
October 9, 2042	Discovers cure for cancer ….

God knows about each boy and girl before they are formed in the womb. He knows about our brothers, sisters and friends. He gives us the gift of making our choices, and is there to help us choose right, if we ask Him. He knows the choices we will make.

ÀPÈKẸ́ LOVES TO SING, SKIP AND DANCE
LIKE THESE GIRLS IN THE PICTURES.

Illustration 17: Girl singing

Illustration 18: Girl Skipping

Illustration 19: Girl Dancing

SHE JOINS THE CHOIR IN CHURCH
WHEN SHE GETS INTO PRIMARY SCHOOL.

Illustration 20: Choir

Her younger brother is called Fẹ́mi, which is short for Olúfẹ́mi; meaning God loves me. He loves football. Her older brother, Àrèmú, likes to play the drum. He was very good in the primary school assembly drumming team and later became the church drummer. Parents can tell what their children are good at quite early in life.

(Parent, encourage them in their natural talent. Read Proverbs 22:6)

> *Train up a child in the way that he should go (and in keeping with his individual gift or bent), and when he is old, he will not depart from it.*

> *-Proverbs 22:6 - The Amplified Bible*

As you grow up loving God, the love and peace in you will be seen by those around you by God's grace. Amen. You will be a blessing. Àpèkẹ́ is a blessing.
Like this girl, she reads to her younger sister while her mum does some household chores.

HER SISTER SAYS SHE'S A TREASURE.

Illustration 21: Girl Reading to sister

So are Hannah, Fẹmi and John. They help at home. Do you?

Illustration 22: This is Hanna making the bed

Fẹ́mi is picking beans, removing stone and chaff. Oh, load of fibre!

Illustration 23: Fẹ́mi picking the beans

This is John putting the trash bag away

Illustration 24: John with the trash bag

Fẹ́mi is helping with washing of plates

Illustration 25: Fẹ́mi standing on a stool, washing plates

JESUS IS HAPPY WHEN CHILDREN PRAY

Àpèkẹ́ does what her Mummy, Aunties, and of course Daddy say. She prays to God like this little girl and cleans her teeth when she wakes up.

Illustration 26: Girl praying

JESUS IS HAPPY WHEN WE HONOUR OUR PARENTS

Her friend, Eileen is Irish. Àpèké̩ and Eileen have different ways of greeting their parents, but both filled with love. Eileen says good morning to her parents with a smile. Do you greet Mummy and Daddy when you wake up? How do you greet them?

Do you greet older people with courtesy and treat everyone with grace?

Àpèké̩ goes on her knees to say good morning to her parents, like her sister (and all good Yorùbá girls).

The way to learn a good habit is by example. ☺☺☺.

Illustration 27: Àpèké̩'s sister greeting mum

JESUS IS HAPPY WHEN WE CLEAN OUR ENVIRONMENT

Àpèkẹ́ learns to sweep the compound very clean like her sister.

**Illustration 28a: Àpèkẹ́'s sister
sweeping the floor with a broom**

**Illustration 28b: Boy
cleaning with a vaccum**

She goes to Sunday school, listens carefully to the teachers, and learns some new songs about Jesus, Father God and The Holy Spirit; like '<u>Jesus loves me this I know</u>' . Here it is in Tonic Sol-fa

Jesus loves me, this I know
so fa mi re mi so so

For The Bible tells me so
la la doh2 la la so so

Little Ones to Him belong
so fa mi re mi so so

They are weak but He is strong
la la so doh mi re doh

Yes Jesus loves me
so mi so la doh2

Yes Jesus loves me
so mi doh mi re

Yes Jesus loves me
so mi so la doh2

The Bible tells me so
la so doh mi re doh
Now in Yorùbá

Jesu fẹ mi, mo mọ bẹẹ
so fa mi re mi so so

Bibeli lo sọ fun mi
la la doh2 la la so so

Tirẹ l'awọn ọmọde
so fa mi re mi so so

Nwọn ko l'agbara Oun ni
la la so doh mi re doh

Ah, Jesu fẹ mi
so mi so la doh2

Ah, Jesu fẹ mi
so mi doh mi re

Ah, Jesu fẹ mi
so mi so la doh2

Bibeli sọ fun mi
la so doh mi re doh

Note: Tonic Sol-fa here goes 'doh re mi fa so la ti doh2'

JESUS LOVES LITTLE CHILDREN

All children like to try new things. Sometimes the little one would try to do new things and taste new things

Illustration 29: Jesus with children

Illustration 30: Baby with toy in mouth

And the toddlers of course like to try out a toy

Illustration 31: Toddlers with tricycle

Illustration 32: Àpèké trying out her new tricycle

CHILDREN ARE REWARDS FROM ON HIGH

Àpèké̩ decides to try out her hands on her mother's sewing machine! OUCH

Illustration 32: Old hand operated machine

CHILDREN ARE PRECIOUS IN GODS SIGH

Àpèké̩ sews her finger! Ah, It's very painful.

Illustration 33: Cry Cry Cry

Àpèkẹ́ made a mistake. She's not perfect.

Have you ever made a mistake?

Everyone makes mistakes

The important thing is to learn from it, say sorry, and not do it again Better still Ask your Mum or Dad for guidance or advice before you do something new. Learn from other people's mistakes

Ask your teacher or parents to explain how to do a task, or whether you are old enough. Read Bible Stories and learn good examples. Do them!

ASSIGNMENT:

1. Give Àpèkẹ́'s sisters names and read the story again

2. Tell your friend the story

LESSONS TO LEARN

- Jesus loves and treasures everyone. John 3:16
- He plans for each child to be a blessing
- You learn good songs in Sunday School
- Be careful trying new things.

When you want to try your new toy, have an adult around and **don't play with Auntie or Mummy's sewing machine!**

PRAYER TO APPRECIATE AND COMMIT TO CHRIST

Dear heavenly Father, I thank you for loving me even before I was made in my mum. Your love for children and adults is so great you sent Your Sinless Son Jesus to die on the cross in our place – for all the wrong we do. But You raised Him up, and He lives forever now. Please forgive me my wrong – all of them. Lord Jesus, please come into my life. Help me love you, please you, tolerate and truly love other people. Please send your Holy Spirit to give me the power to live for you. Amen.

TELL someone you've prayed this prayer and go to a Bible believing Church. Ask your parent to take you. Buy a Bible and Daily Devotional Notes from a Christian Bookshop. Read your Bible DAY and Night. Ask for assistance if these will be a struggle to buy. Free resources Online for families by other authors include

Word for Today https://www.ucb.co.uk>wordforyou ;
Our Daily Bread https://odb.org ;
Holy Bible different versions https://biblegateway.com

God is able to keep you, even when you've made a mistake. Stay close to Him, following in Christ's steps by The Holy Spirit.

About the Author

Mofoluṣọ Ọmọbọla Monisọla Rosanwo. Praise The Lord. Sinner saved by grace, cleansed by the blood of Jesus. Kept by His power and called to point people, especially children to Christ, The Mighty Helper. Hails from Ipetu-Ijesha, Nigeria; preceded into eternal rest by loving husband, Dr Emmanuel Olufẹmi Rosanwo, with a Super Mother-in-law, lovely Children, Children in Christ and Grandsons, Aunties, Uncles, Brothers, Sisters, Nieces, Nephews, In Laws, Cousins and a large family; plus faithful friends, good neighbours, co-labourers, of all or no faiths; who have prayed for or supported and tremendously helped her. May God bless us and all readers - at the foot of the Cross. Amen, in The Mighty Name of Jesus.

Room at the Cross for you and me

Illustration 34:The Author and her late spouse

ALL GLORY TO THE LORD!

Printed in the United States
by Baker & Taylor Publisher Services